Paul & family

Enjoy

ODD SOCKS
and other oddities

HUW JONES

Huw Jones.

Illustrations: Jenny Fell

bwthyn
GWASG Y BWTHYN

© Huw Jones
Gwasg y Bwthyn 2009

© Illustrations: Jenny Fell

ISBN 9-781904845-83-6

All rights reserved.
No part of this book may be reproduced or transmitted in any form or by any means, electronic or mechanical, including photocopying, recording, or by any information storage and retrieval system, without permission in writing from the publisher.

The publisher acknowledges the financial support
of the Welsh Books Council.

Published and printed by Gwasg y Bwthyn, Caernarfon

CONTENTS

When I get to Heaven 7
Whatever the Weather 8
Walls 9
Tortoise News 10
The Giraphant 11
The Crunchy Wunchy Creature 13
The Cabbage Song 14
Spells for Odd Occasions 15
Sighting 16
Riddle 17
Reverend Din 18
Poem 20
Old Austin 21
Odd Socks 22
Magellan's Mice 24
Mac the Packman 28
Lullaby 29

Limericks 30
If I went to Africa 31
If Bees Make Honey 32
How Many ? 33
Going Nuts 34
Get Away 35
Fusspot Fanny 36
Find Me 37
Carpets ? 38
Birthday 40
Around the World with . . . 41
Africa 44
Abandoned Sonnet 45

For my daughters
Seren Haf and Tirion Awel
and in memory of my mother
Heulwen Jones

ACKNOWLEDGEMENTS

Poetry Wales 25 Years (Seren 1990). Editor: Cary Archard.
Birdsong (Seren 2002). Editor: Dewi Roberts.
Thoughts Like an Ocean (Pont 1997). Editors: Neil Nuttall and Andy Hawkins.
Look Out! (Pont 1999). Editors: Neil Nuttall and Andy Hawkins.
Second Thoughts (Pont 2003). Editors: Neil Nuttall and Andy Hawkins.

When I get to Heaven

When I get to heaven
will I have a coat-peg
marked with my name
and a picture of a pineapple ?

Will I learn again
to share crayons and paint,
build towns with others
of cardboard and glue ?

Will I learn again
to measure the world with wonder,
marvel at jars of pond-water
sparkling with spawn ?

When I get to heaven
will I sing a new song,
learn again the lessons
that living has erased ?

Whatever the Weather

Ice-cream weather, chocolate flake,
    Candyfloss and pop;
Mince-pie weather, sizzling bangers,
    Bowls of Dracula soup.

Picnic-weather, water-slides,
    Bikes and climbing frames;
Jigsaw weather, dressing-up,
    Cartoons and video games.

T-shirt weather, cool new trainers,
    Shades and baseball caps;
Welly weather, striped umbrellas,
    Scarves and bobble-hats.

Bunny weather, wobbly lambs,
    Bogs of burping frogs;
Penguin weather, flying reindeer,
    Soggy cats and dogs.

There's *such* a lot of weather;
It's bound to last for ever!

Walls

Walls have faces, broad or narrow,
Sullen under smoke and shadow,
Grumpy granite, fiery brick,
Seaside pink that makes you sick.
Walls surround us from Day One
Their patterns fading in the sun.

Walls have ears, hidden corners
Listen to our every whisper:
He said this, she said that –
Walls are fond of a little chat.
Ruins are walls that leaned too long
Trying to understand our song.

Walls have eyes, round or square,
Make us wonder why they stare
As windows watch us come and go
And weep for summers long ago.
Hall and mansion gazing west
Reflect the setting sun's request.

Walls have voices, grumble and groan,
Usually when we're alone,
They like to play our conversations
Recorded in stone for generations.
Towers tell us with their chimes
There's only time for one last rhyme.

Tortoise News

We are a pair of living stones
   The Great One made us so,
We weren't designed to dash about
   As if there's no tomorrow.

We crawl around in Lilliput
   Nibble on lettuce or fruit,
We dawdle along to the library
   Only to find it shut.

We take our time to read and write
   Fill in the crossword clues,
Our answer to winter is hibernate
   With a copy of *Tortoise News*.

Small and slow, it's just not fair,
   The Big Ones overlook us,
Though we can outwit any hare
   And win the longest race.

The Giraphant

(For William, Samuel and Amy)

The elusive, gentle Giraphant
   Has a strange ginormous shape,
Nothing quite like it has ever been seen
   From Cairo to the Cape.

On legs broad as baobab trees
   It travels farther than far,
With a neck long as moonbeams
   It browses among the stars.

The Giraphant is fond of games
   Especially Hide and Seek,
It seeks a deep and tangly place
   And hides there for a week.

Herds of tourists on safari
   Wait with fancy cameras,
You know who lies in the shade
   Playing Snakes and Adders.

It likes to relax when the sun goes down
    At a favourite waterhole,
Four and twenty pints of mud
    And soggy sausage rolls.

Those who camp near Nxai Pan
    Relate their tales of wonder,
They've heard the creature clean its teeth
    And snore like distant thunder.

The Crunchy Wunchy Creature

I met a creature in the wood
    Where all such creatures lurk,
Its many eyes were Mint Imperials
    Which glistened in the dark.

    A giant humbug was his head
        And truffle was his tum,
    His legs were made of liquorice
        His bum of bubble-gum.

        'Hello,' he boomed, 'I'm Crunchy Wunchy,
            Have a chocolate finger,
        My toes are rather tasty too
            They're made of barley sugar.'

            'I'm sure you're very sweet,' I said,
                'But what if you eat me?'
            I ran away and I'm glad to say
                He couldn't run for toffee!

The Cabbage Song

One two
cabbage to chew

three four
run for the door

five six
time to be sick

seven eight
back to my plate

nine ten
cabbage again

repeat !

Spells for Odd Occasions

I

abacus, abacus,
one, two, three,
turn this person ★
into a flea

abacus, abacus,
eight, nine, ten,
turn this person
back again.

II

quercetum, quercetum,
royal trees,
turn your leaves
into gold for me

quercetum, quercetum,
royal trees,
wads of fivers
will do nicely.

III

Corvus corone
solitary crow,
show me from high
shapes of tomorrow

Corvus corone
solitary crow,
now take me back
to streets I know

★ The person's name recited here
will make them blush from ear to ear.

Sighting

Powis Castle Park

A stag of sandstone
peeps through the trees
keeping the herd from harm

We gaze
like portraits in the Long Gallery
at deer grazing under oaks

We inch forward
like frightened foot-soldiers
to deer standing in pools of sunlight

    Twigs crack
    antlers flash like swords
    hooves drum the frozen ground

    We sigh
    as though our hopes and dreams
    had slipped away for good

    Today
    we saw the deer running
    in a world of sunshine and snow

Riddle

I am the space between stars
   sky's unfinished score;
I am the music of rock and pool
   shadows on a hidden shore.

I am the dance of the Admirals
   on banks of Lady's Smock;
I am the parting at the gate
   the kiss as lovers lock.

I am the breath of orchard mist
   shrouding an empty swing;
I am the song of sleeping birds
   an owl on muffled wing.

I am the weight of a winter sky
   sheets of snow on the fen;
I am the tracks across the common
   after the last amen.

Reverend Din

The Very Reverend Rumbletum Din
Was preaching another sermon on sin
When all of a sudden a distant trumpet
Seemed to echo from the pulpit.
The congregation shook with laughter
At their cleric's strange disorder :
An unpredictable musical middle
Blaring forth a rumtum tiddle.

The Very Noisy Reverend Din
Was cursed by wind and a double chin,
His tummy would rumble and tumble at will
In spite of a diet and various pills.
He woke up baby in its buggy
With whistles and hoots of a jamboree;
He startled Granny in her chair
With a tinny old tune from a travelling fair.

The Very Versatile Reverend Din
Was able to play a few bars of Haydn
Which came in handy at the summer fête
When raising funds for a new church gate.
People came from near and far
To hear his growing repertoire,
They started swaying in the pews
To jazz, pop, rhythm and blues.

The Very Reverend Rumbletum Din
Preached a number of sermons on sin
Accompanied by his famous middle,
A distant trumpet and second fiddle.
The congregation at Saint Dan's
Grew quite fond of their clergyman,
His sermons no longer filled them with dread
As no one could hear a word he said.

Poem stood on a small hill,
four friends together
watching the world below

until one hot afternoon
when **o** rolled down the slope
and bounced into a p**o**nd.

P disappeared in a puff of smoke
spinning like a firework
up into s**p**ace.

On a blustery day
e got carried away
at the end of a child's kit**e**

leaving **m** on the hill
to **m**ope on its own
for **o**, **p** and **e**

Old Austin

Put out to grass,
abandoned for a faster breed
that races along motorways.
In the field's workshop
ferns slowly spray him green,
rain refills the tank.

Some nights
when a bright moon
switches on his headlights,
a badger squats behind the wheel
and taxies home a few owls
tipsy after a barn dance.

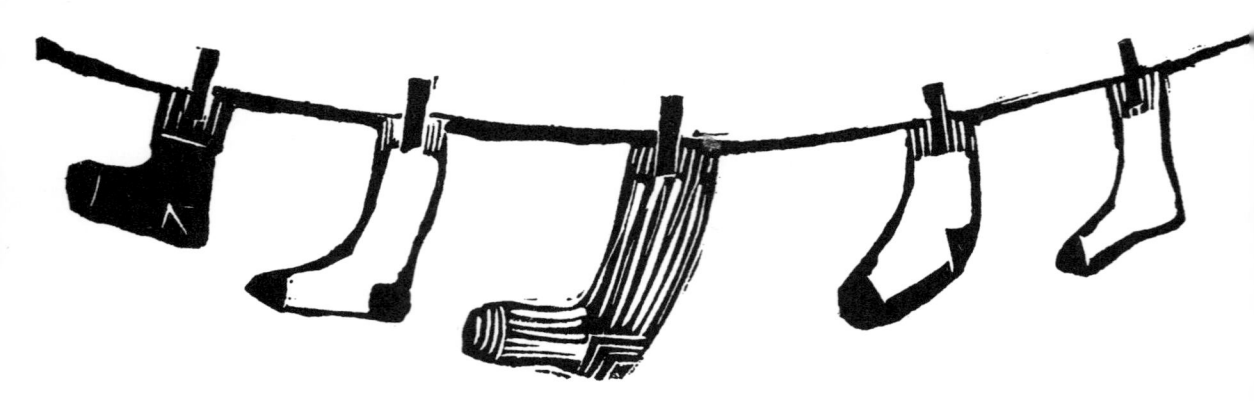

Odd Socks

Where do they go, those odd socks,
   Leaving us a laughing-stock ?
Long or short, pink or brown,
   Disappear when we're in town.

Do Borrowers in dusty corners
   Drag them down beneath the floor,
Unravel each to make a blanket,
   Curtains, mats and tiny hats ?

Do dogs run off with them like bones
   Bury them under soil and stones ?
Is it a case for sniffer-dogs
   To search the wood in rain and fog ?

Do swallows swoop in summertime
 Snatch them off the washing line ?
Are there nests from here to Hull
 Designed in trendy pure new wool ?

Is there a boat beyond the rocks
 Trawling the bay for missing socks
Left behind on empty beaches
 With half-eaten sandwiches ?

Is there a castle under padlock
 Rooms full of assorted socks
Collected by some mad professor
 Researching colour, size and odour ?

Yes they're odd, but let's be fair,
 They're only odd when not a pair.
Is a sock that's left its partner
 Any odder than the other ?

I merely ask, like Socrates,
 Fond of socks that reached his knees.
Perhaps we'll find them, those odd socks,
 In an Odd Sock Shop in Vladivostok.

Magellan's Mice

(On board *Victoria* 1519-22)

These are days we fear the most
a scurvy crew grey as ghosts,
the look-out sleeping in despair
the vessel listing leagues from nowhere.
They come to find our hidy-holes
scramble about in the dark holds:

with lantern swinging, a stinking sailor
hopes to knife a little squealer,
sick to death of toasted leather
plates of sawdust and putrid water,
his long summer whiskers twitching
at the thought of rodent roasting.

We can always find some food
regardless of our longitude,
snouts steer us into crannies
for dry crumbs of bread and cheese,
an almond prized from the captain's cabin,
a raisin snatched from a bearded chin!

We are the squeaking stowaways
born to explore beyond the bay,
sneaked on board in a broken barrel
to satisfy our taste for travel,
left familiar harbour runs
sailed toward the setting sun.

Fiesta days of play and plenty
casks of ale to drown an army,
a lively jig below deck
mating behind a flour sack,
a quick coupling in the galley
high-pitched fun on the high sea!

Always babies — six in a litter,
blind and deaf they huddle together
safe in a secret nest of wool
lined with a necktie lost in a squall,
nursed behind an oak panel
cradled in a creaking caravel.

Youngsters like to hear our tales
of quaysides quivering with fish and sails,
canaries in cages singing on stalls
melons larger than cannon balls,
ships of stone that seem to swim
in a haze of heat and orange blossom.

They learn of twisted olive trees
standing in line like mutineers,
barns of grain moored on pillars
to hinder hungry scamperers,
the far sierras, a jagged saw,
our cousin caught in a wildcat's jaws.

We are the scurrying multitudes
at home on every latitude,
tenants of mountain, marsh and harbour,
dusty towers and city cellars.
Explorers of the world's terrain
nibbling grain on the Spanish main.

We are the furry seafarers
gnawing our way through rotten timbers,
scratching about in silk and silver
sniffing around in cloves and ginger.
We live to eat and multiply,
our brief crusade before we die.

These are days we fear the most,
caught, skewered and served as roast,
the ragged crew changing watches
staring out for birds and branches.
Prayers to the Virgin lift on the swell
to save them from this peaceful hell.

We peep at sunset after sunset
ebbing sky bright as a parrot.
Someone is playing the crumhorn again,
someone has muttered his last amen.
Tierra! Tierra! they cry in their sleep
as we drift northwest on the starlit deep.

Mac the Packman

He came with showers and rainbows
    laden with pack and news,
ribbons, dainties and gossip
    none of the folk could refuse.

One night at the Wtra Wen
    Evan and Marged Siôn
were shown the wares he carried
    and knew he'd leave at dawn.

They whispered of the wonders
    but had no money to pay,
so gave him a bed in the garden
    under a quilt of clay.

'Hast seen old Mac the packman?'
    asked many a wife and maid,
'He promised me a paisley shawl
    and shirting trimmed with braid.'

Lullaby

Lanes are lost
beneath the leaves
my child
beneath the leaves
and swallows part
with speed and grace
under an amber sky.

The ragged trees
have turned to mist
my child
turned to mist
and badgers leave
their secret beds
to hunt in hooting woods.

Stars are steps
above the hill
my child
above the hill
and moon a slide
for you to slip
with animals and birds.

Limericks

There was an old lady from Skye
Who put chilli in apple pie;
   At the harvest supper
    She watched them splutter,
The naughty old lady of Skye.

          There was a young girl from Rhyl
          Who went out with a boy called Phil;
             On a ride at the fair
              She was sick in his hair,
          The giddy young girl from Rhyl.

There was a young farmer from Foel
Had a rather painful boil;
   He walked like a clown
    And couldn't sit down,
The funny young farmer of Foel.

          A studious worm from Hay
          Ate nothing but books all day;
             On a diet of fiction
              He improved his diction,
          The eloquent worm from Hay.

If I went to Africa

I'd write a trumpet fanfare
For elephants to play;
I'd write a book of jokes
For hyenas to laugh all day.

    I'd sell new pin-stripe suits
    For zebras to look well-dressed;
    I'd sell new spotty jumpers
    For leopards to look their best.

        I'd teach a pair of giraffes
        To waltz between the trees;
        I'd teach a class of snakes
        To recite their ABC.

            I'd open a sauna for hippos
            To wash away the mud;
            I'd open a beauty salon
            So wart-hogs feel they're loved.

                I'd start a taxi-service
                For monkeys to travel in style;
                But I'd never, ever start
                A crèche for crocodiles.

If Bees Make Honey

If bees make honey
   In a busy hive,
Do ants make marmalade
   From nine 'til five ?

Do ladybirds make jam
   In the flower-bed ?
Do spiders make syrup
   In the garden shed ?

Do beetles make chutney
   In the compost heap ?
Do moths make mustard
   When we're fast asleep ?

If bees sold the honey
   They made in their hive,
Would they pack their combs
   And head for St. Ives ?

How Many ?

How many clouds are caught in a storm ?
How many insects fly in a swarm ?

How many worms does a blackbird eat ?
How many horses try to bleat ?

How many spines on a hedgehog's back ?
How many sleepers on a railway track ?

How many snails does a post van crush ?
How many snowmen turn to slush ?

How many spiders hang in the shed ?
How many ants like gingerbread ?

How many bluebells make a pond ?
How many bees in the great beyond ?

How many questions can I ask today ?
How many answers rhyme with hurray ?

Going Nuts

Waking after winter sleep
To skip, to leap, to scamper,
Fribble about in sunbeams
Raid my picnic hamper.

Tag in the leaves, hide and seek,
Climb my favourite tree,
Chase the birds then chase my tail
'Til I'm getting dizzy

But now I'm feeling bored
Playing on a woodland stage,
So if you could excuse me
I'm off to another page.

Get Away

Zoom away to Zanzibar
   Drive a racing car:

Breakfast in the south of France
   Dinner in Japan
Tea and cake in Argentina
   Supper in Sudan.

        Step on board a motor-boat
           Cruise along the coast:

        Leaping with the dolphins
           Sliding with the seals
        Drifting with the jelly-fish
           A walrus at the wheel.

                Dream beneath the duvet
                   Tour the Milky Way:

                Kick off on Jupiter
                   Pass the ball on Mars
                Score a try on Saturn
                   Bring home a cup of stars.

Fusspot Fanny

Fusspot Fanny in her cot
Never liked the toys she got

Fusspot Fanny went to school
Five minutes early as a rule

Fusspot Fanny played with her food
Cabbage caused a family feud

Fusspot Fanny tidied her bedroom
Every morning and afternoon

                        Fusspot Fanny lived on her own
                        Other people made her moan

                        Fusspot Fanny scolded the rain
                        For leaving streaks on the window pane

                        Fusspot Fanny cleaned the house
                        Died of shock when she saw a mouse

                        Fusspot Fanny told Saint Peter
                        Heaven should be a little neater.

Find me

I'm found in Wales and England,
    Across the Irish Sea,
I can't be found in Scotland
    Spain or Italy.

I'll never leave Teresa
    Melanie or Gwen,
Peter's lost without me
    And so are Kev and Ben.

Fasting turns to feasting
    When I cast my spell,
Firs that turn to fires
    Will surely ring some bells.

I'm in the middle of poetry
    In metre and in rhyme,
I'm at the start of everything
    And at the end of time.

Carpets ?

Hamsters squeak in the glove compartment
Wait to escape at any moment

Rabbits jump about like fleas
Nibble the seats' upholstery

Cats purr like warm engines
Idling at a busy junction

Dogs are content to nod or natter
Often make a reliable chauffeur

Parrots are terrible back-seat drivers
"Turn right, turn left, pull over."

Canaries sing on every journey
Of tropical islands across the sea

Spiders are masters of illusion
Crack the windscreen just for fun

Snakes are best kept out of sight
Or worn as scarves on frosty nights

Sometimes there's no room for Granny
Who sits on the roof-rack knitting a cardi

A car of furry and feathered friends
Is sure to drive you round the bend.

Birthday

It's someone's birthday today,
   I wonder whose it is ?
There's icing on the hill
   And candles of prickly gorse.

The wind has invitations
   To post around the block;
Hazel has yellow ribbons
   Holly an emerald frock.

The gulls at Station Terrace
   Play musical chimney-pots,
They blow their party whistles
   Chase their paper hats.

When Mr Moon, Magician,
   Tip-toes up the stairs,
He leaves a purse of silver
   A window signed with stars.

Around the World with . . .

Myrtle

Once upon a turtle the earth was flat,
flat as a plate, flat as a cow-pat.
A flaming chariot climbed the heavens
pulled by a team of gleaming stallions.
If you travelled west to the farthest stream
you'd find them drinking in a moonlit dream.
Hills, valleys, trees and plants,
rested on a herd of elephants
who stood on the back of a giant turtle
(for want of a rhyme we'll call her Myrtle)
swimming an ocean's shoreless abyss
swimming for as long as forever is.

Mathematicians

The ancient Greeks were puzzled by
mysteries of earth and sky.
Why could no-one reach the horizon ?
Why create such a cruel illusion ?

Bright as mice in dark bazaars
they studied patterns of turning stars
the slowly disappearing ships
a full moon's coppery eclipse.
Eratosthenes, beside the Nile,
(there's a name to make you smile)
measured the earth's circumference
with poles, shadows, angles and distance.

Magellan

In 1519 Magellan's fleet
sailed from Spain in summer heat.
A brochure then would hardly mention
risks of crossing unchartered ocean,
gales, shipwreck, mutiny,
bowls of sawdust, a mouse for tea;
leagues of nothing but sky and sea
a heaving grave for those with scurvy.
They promised God to visit shrines
if He would save them from the brine.
Only one ship and many tears
to tell of a trip that lasted three years.

Astronauts

The man in the moon was out to lunch
when *Eagle* landed with a nervous crunch.
He'd have liked a little natter
about the lack of local weather,
the landscape being rather bare –
a crater here, a crater there.
Beyond a dusty, lunar sea
earth is hanging silently,
the fruit of all biology
safe in the arms of gravity.
Who could ever fail to care
for such a prize at creation's fair ?

• • •

Africa

A for Allah whom a Muslim reveres
   with Arabic prayers in a mosque in Algiers

F for famine the grim dictator
   in countries gripped by drought and war

R for rains reviving grain
   clouds migrating across the plains

I for insects scuttling through dust
   whining and dining on swarms of tourists

C for cities from Cape to Cairo
   where money speaks the local lingo

A for acacia, a toothpick tree
   where lions lie between dinner and tea.

I've always wanted to complete a sonnet
But somehow never seemed to get it right,
Distracted easily by golf and cricket
Or frames of snooker late into the night.
The Unfinished Sonnets of Yours Truly
Lie in a drawer like gloves on summer days;
Perhaps, when I'm decomposing slowly,
A friend will publish them to lavish praise.
I start each one in optimistic mood
(Last week I wrote ten lines about a gnu)
But thoughts inevitably turn to food.
Time for tea. I'll leave the couplet to you . . .

Abandoned Sonnet XVII